Original title:
The Secret of the Living Room

Copyright © 2025 Creative Arts Management OÜ
All rights reserved.

Author: Mariana Leclair
ISBN HARDBACK: 978-1-80587-130-9
ISBN PAPERBACK: 978-1-80587-600-7

The Heart of Everyday Shelters

In the corner stands a chair,
It wiggles when you sit and stare.
The cushions hum a tune so light,
Each squeak a giggle, pure delight.

Beneath the lamp, a cat does nap,
With dreams of chasing, oh what a trap!
The books all whisper tales so grand,
Of worlds outside this cozy land.

Unraveled Threads of Familiarity

A blanket toss upon the floor,
Like spaghetti, it sprawls and soars.
Remote controls play hide and seek,
The couch is where we laugh and peek.

Old socks peek from beneath the chair,
Their mismatched pairs, beyond compare.
A tangle of laughter fills the air,
In this room, there's magic to share.

Silence Between the Shelves

Dust bunnies dance in the night,
Whispers of stories, taking flight.
The shelves are stacked with all things odd,
A rubber chicken, a tiny trod.

Behind the books, a mystery lies,
Giant marshmallows? We'll improvise!
Each corner creaks, a voice so wise,
In this room, humor never dies.

Muffled Dreams in Quiet Spaces

A pillow fort, arching sky-high,
With giggles buried, oh my, oh my!
The laughter echoes, no need for sound,
In this cozy nook, joy is found.

The clock ticks softly, time stands still,
While snack crumbs gather, what a thrill!
Each hidden spot is a world anew,
In our sanctuary, laughter grew.

Memories Intertwined with Dust

In corners forgotten, they weave and they twist,
Old socks and old toys, how could I resist?
Whispers of laughter, they tickle the air,
Dust bunnies jigging, with each little flare.

A couch full of stories, some silly, some bold,
Embraced by the cushions where secrets unfold.
The upholstery chuckles at tales of the past,
As we dive in the depths of memories amassed.

Where Time Slips Between Cushions

A remote plays hide-and-seek, what a game!
Lost in the depths, it's always the same.
The room hums with secrets and sparks of delight,
As popcorn kernels dance under soft, dim light.

Each pillow a portal to worlds yet unseen,
Adventures we have, oh, if they could glean!
Time winks from the clock, it twirls and it bends,
In this kingdom of laughter, where the fun never ends.

Secrets under the Coffee Table

Beneath the surface, a mess hides with glee,
Magazines piled high, as far as the eye can see.
Old receipts whisper tales of trips we forgot,
While crumbs from last week munch on memories caught.

The coffee table creaks like an old jazz tune,
Each scratch telling stories of afternoons,
And if you listen closely, you might just find,
The echoes of laughter left trailing behind.

Reflections of Life in Frames

The walls laugh with memories caught in a glance,
Snapshots of chaos, the perfect dance.
Each frame is a giggle, a wink from the past,
Capturing moments, too funny to last.

We gather 'round photos, our faces aglow,
With shadows of pranks and antics on show.
The living room buzzes with stories to share,
In this gallery of giggles, we breathe in the air.

Roots of Bonding in Unseen Vibes.

In the corner, where the cat naps,
Laughter lurks beneath the snaps.
Sticky notes claim the fridge's face,
While chaos swirls in a merry race.

Socks unwound, a carpet trail,
Stories laughed, no need to fail.
In mismatched shoes, we dance around,
With goofy cheers, our joy is found.

Chairs that squeak, confront the day,
With every spill, we find our way.
Crumbs of laughter join the fray,
In this haven, we choose to play.

Whispers Behind Closed Doors

Giggles hide where the cushions sigh,
As secrets float, and dreams can fly.
Pillow forts construct our reign,
While mischief stirs like salty grain.

Under tables, plans unfold,
With whispers sweet, and tales retold.
A closet's dark, a pirate's loot,
Where socks turn spies in search of fruit.

Fuzzy slippers on the run,
Chasing shadows just for fun.
These walls embrace our silly plot,
Where every squeak is laughter's jot.

Hushed Echoes in Cozy Corners

In the nooks, where secrets dwell,
Echoes of laughter weave their spell.
Blankets heap like clouds of cheer,
Worn out jokes bring everyone near.

Chips and dip, a feast of mirth,
Every giggle reveals its worth.
In quiet corners, joy can bloom,
Making magic in a cozy room.

Mismatched mugs on the lam,
Sharing life like a fevered jam.
With every burst, the silence bends,
As humor mingles, and warmth descends.

Shadowed Corners of Comfort

In shadowed nooks where shadows play,
Our laughter weaves a bright bouquet.
Hidden treasures spill in jest,
Surprises wait for the very best.

A dog that snorts, a cat that purrs,
Each gentle noise becomes my cure.
With snacks piled high like a mountain's peak,
We dive right in, no need to sneak.

In creaky chairs, we spin our tales,
Through all our wins and epic fails.
The loving bonds in whispers thrive,
In cozy spots, we feel alive.

Reticent Whispers of Home

In corners where cushions conspire,
And dust bunnies frolic, a secret choir.
Laughter spills from a worn-out chair,
As socks escape from laundry's snare.

Bernie the cat, with pompous pride,
Perched on the TV, he won't be denied.
The remote goes missing, oh, what a plight!
We check on the sofa, let's hope it's not bite.

The fridge hums tunes of forgotten food,
A salsa of leftovers, oh so crude.
Mismatched mugs gather round with glee,
As tales unfold like spilled tea.

In this sanctuary, where silence falls,
A dance of chaos in the echoing halls.
We hide from chores with TV's embrace,
In laughter's embrace, we find our place.

A Ritual of Remembrance

Gather 'round, it's that time again,
For stories of Grandma and her old pen.
How she knitted a sweater so snug and weird,
That even the moths found it quite revered.

A game of charades begins with a twist,
As Dad roles a cupcake on his little fist.
With flour on noses and smiles so wide,
A little bit of chaos on this whimsical ride.

Silly dances erupt in the dim-lit room,
While shadows waltz, igniting the gloom.
Pasta from Tuesday makes a grand return,
In the microwave, we watch and discern.

Echoes of laughter bounce off the walls,
As we reminisce in these friendly halls.
Home is the canvas where memories blend,
Each silly tale echoes, a giggling friend.

The Unraveled Comfort of Presence

Boots by the door, a welcome sight,
A jumble of shoes, left in delight.
"Who needs an umbrella?" shouts Uncle Joe,
As he dashes outside, like a pro in the snow.

The couch swallows all who dare to sit,
Crumbs and snacks make it feel quite fit.
We ponder life's meaning over chips and dip,
While Mom rolls her eyes at every last quip.

Fairy lights twinkle, a soft, warm glow,
While bubbles of laughter inevitably flow.
We debate who makes the best paper plane,
And blame the dog when they fly in vain.

In this cozy cocoon of silly disputes,
We find our treasure in reconvened roots.
Through playful banter and loving cheers,
The warmth of togetherness calms all fears.

A Journey through Upholstered Dreams

Cushions whisper tales of yarn,
As the cat conducts a velvet charm.
Remote controls, the navigator's seat,
Losing socks to the sofa's heartbeat.

The popcorn pops like slippery dreams,
While laughter bounces off the seams.
A kingdom ruled by blanket fort,
Where every game's a royal sport.

Lost in cushions, we take a dive,
In this jungle, we feel alive.
The TV laughs at our weekend quests,
As we conquer snacks with fervent zest.

And when the light begins to fade,
We recall the couch brigade we laid.
In this space of warmth and fun,
The journey ends, but we're just begun.

Flickers of Warmth

A lamp flickers like a playful tease,
Chasing shadows with a gentle breeze.
The cat leaps high, then he lands with flair,
Claiming the spot in the softest chair.

Crumbs collect like little treasures,
Each scattered laugh marks our pleasures.
The flicks of light dance, twirl, and spin,
While the dog rolls with a goofy grin.

Crazy stories woven in the air,
As we tangle our feet without a care.
Remote battles, who turns the channel?
This is not war; it's our merry panel.

The rug holds secrets of spilled delights,
With tickling moments on winter nights.
In the glow of joy, all seems just right,
Wrapped in laughter, we soar to new heights.

Emerging Patterns in Stillness

In the silence, a snore does rise,
Matching the buzz of TV skies.
A quilt drapes us in silly schemes,
Where laughter blooms in patterned dreams.

Old magazines scatter, tales untold,
Each page crinkles like secrets bold.
A plush fortress built for the bold,
Where heroes save the shy and the old.

Sipping tea, watching antics unfold,
The chair creaks like it's filled with gold.
Doodles dance upon the table's edge,
As we spill stories from a friendly pledge.

In this quiet, fun emerges bright,
Turning every moment into delight.
With laughter echoing off the wall,
Patterns form as we have a ball.

Hidden in Plain Sight

Underneath the cushions, what do we find?
A treasure map drawn by a curious mind.
Remote controls and crayons entwine,
In our cozy chaos, everything's fine.

The closet swallows forgotten shoes,
While the couch supports our joyful muse.
Peeking behind, there's more to uncover,
Adventures waiting for every lover.

Here lies the place where goofiness reigns,
Where laughter washes away all the pains.
Moments captured, silly faces abide,
In this realm, we all dart and glide.

So stay awhile, let joy ignite,
In shadows where giggles take flight.
With every glance, we share this bliss,
In the hide-and-seek we cannot miss.

Constellations on the Floor

In a sea of snacks and shoes,
The floor becomes a map to choose.
Crisps like stars, a crumbly moon,
Lost in laughter, we'll find it soon.

Under blankets, we create our sky,
Sipping soda, as time flies by.
Each spill a supernova shines,
This universe, where joy aligns.

Couch cushions act as space debris,
Drifting dreams and wild stories free.
With every giggle, the cosmos grows,
In a galaxy only we suppose.

So here we sit, in cosmic glee,
Laughing at how the snacks flee.
Finding constellations on the floor,
As our laughter echoes forevermore.

The Untold Stories of Soft Chairs

In plush thrones where whispers dwell,
Soft chairs quietly weave their spell.
Pillow fights and tales so bright,
Where secrets hide in plain sight.

Each cushion holds a timeworn joke,
Waiting for the right poke.
Reclined adventures, oh so grand,
In the realm of fabric land.

The corner chair grumbles with age,
As we turn its tales to a page.
With a creak, it shares its plight,
Of movie nights and endless bites.

So take a seat, come share the lore,
Of soft chairs and what's in store.
In laughter's embrace, we'll reminisce,
In cozy corners, it's pure bliss.

In the Heart of Homeliness

Where socks are mismatched, all is well,
In every corner, a tale to tell.
Dust bunnies dance in carefree delight,
A home alive, in joy's own light.

Messy tables hold art divine,
Spilled coffee cups and cheap red wine.
Family photos, crooked frames,
Shout of love in silly names.

The heartbeats echo, with every clatter,
In this warm space, it's all that matters.
With every toast, we share our cheer,
And laugh about the home we steer.

So let the chaos, itself be muse,
In this living room, we can't refuse.
For in the heart of cozy cheer,
We find our joy in our gathered sphere.

Fleeting Glances of Reminisce

A glance at the clock, oh what a race,
Moments fly through this sacred space.
With giggles echoing in our ears,
We hold on tight to the passing years.

Snapshots freeze in a twinkling beam,
Replaying life like a vivid dream.
Movie trailers of yesteryears,
Chasing shadows mixed with cheers.

The flicker of light, a playful tease,
Each memory dances like a gentle breeze.
With every glance, stories unfurl,
In the living room, our joy's pearl.

So let's lift a toast to days gone by,
With laughter and love that will never dry.
In fleeting glances, we remember this,
A tapestry woven in pure bliss.

Disguised in Corner Shadows

In the corner, a cat plots,
A sneaky thief with stealthy thoughts.
Dust bunnies roll like tiny cars,
While the poor lamp dreams of being stars.

Old socks send whispers, 'We once danced!'
In jovial frolic, they seized their chance.
The couch is a ship on a cushion sea,
While remotes hide, designing their spree.

Pillows conspire to keep a secret,
Where snacks are buried, oh so discreet.
The rug giggles underfoot each night,
As lives unfold in morning's light.

Fuzzy memories float around,
As laughter echoes with joy unbound.
In this cozy nook, all's a delight,
Where even the dust feels free to write.

Heartbeats in a Quiet Haven

In silence whispers the heartbeat's tune,
As saggy chairs hum a mellow rune.
A squirrel darts past the window's gaze,
While clocks tick softly in a lazy daze.

Beneath the table, lost treasures hide,
An errant sock, and a cat's great pride.
The carpet sighs beneath playful feet,
While laughter weaves through like a warm sheet.

A mug once filled with coffee bold,
Now holds pens, tales waiting to be told.
Wall art winks, noticing the fun,
In this tranquil zone, where all's begun.

Cushions collide in a soft pillow fight,
As cookies crumble, spreading pure delight.
Amidst the warmth, the spirit lifts,
In this little haven, life's sweetest gifts.

Unraveling Threads of Memory

Threads hang loose from an old recliner,
Tickling the fancies of a loose-lipped designer.
A forgotten teddy, with a fragile smile,
Sits regally on the shelf, all the while.

Under the TV, dust gathers and stirs,
As the popcorn bowl chuckles, recalling its blurs.
The journal giggles as pages unfold,
Spinning yarns of adventures, brave and bold.

Old coasters reminisce of spills and thrills,
Not just a flat disk, but a witness to chills.
Split seams voice stories, of naps gone awry,
In this hallowed nook, time gently takes flight.

Sofa cushions thrum with a hidden beat,
Softly animating the stories they greet.
When dusk settles in, the laughter remains,
In this cherished space, life never wanes.

The Hidden Lives of Objects

A lamp postures like it owns the place,
While a book sighs, revealing its face.
Framed pictures raise conspiratorial brows,
Chatting about their memorable vows.

A remote control dons a wizard's cape,
Channeling magics to keep the tape.
Vases gossip as if time stood still,
Spilling secrets like a cramped-up quill.

The clock, with its hands, does a wavy dance,
While the old chair grumbles about its chance.
Cushions blend, in a theatrical flair,
Holding court with soft giggles wafting in air.

In this space, objects do not lie low,
While the sun spills in with a warm, gentle glow.
In the whispers of walls, we find great cheer,
For what's hidden in plain sight is always near.

The Hushed Magic of Domesticity

In corners where dust bunnies play,
And cushions are dreams tucked away,
A cat with a mission, on the prowl,
Unfolds the day's most delightful scowl.

Underneath the coffee table's reign,
Old magazines whisper tales of grain,
A family of socks, a pair now lost,
Adventures in laundry, what a cost!

The lamp flickers, a light bulb tease,
While popcorn kernels dance with ease,
Laughter spills from the cozy nook,
As everyone searches for their own book.

Mismatched chairs sing a quirky tune,
Waltzing with plates, they're gone by noon,
In the realm of snacks, all rules are bent,
Creating joy is the best intent.

Intrigues Amidst the Knick-Knacks

On a shelf, porcelain clowns stand tall,
Guarding the secrets of the wall,
Curious eyes and crooked grins,
Keep watch for the mischief that begins.

A teapot once deemed fancy and grand,
Now a treasure trove, not quite planned,
Whistles of gossip from spoons and forks,
As they plot against the passing storks.

Behind the vase of wilted blooms,
Lie tales of laughter and household gloom,
A ceramic dog with a charming face,
Mocks the vacuum's relentless chase.

Tangled in yarn, a rogue ball rolls,
Escaping the grasp of nimble trolls,
In the cluttered chaos, joy can thrive,
As households conspire to feel alive.

Once Upon a Settee

Once a settee, plush and grand,
Held dreams of a faraway land,
Cried on by cushions, snug and tight,
At night, it gleamed with starlit light.

Beneath that fabric, stories dwell,
Adventures shared, tales to tell,
With snacks tucked away, oh so sly,
As shadows dance and time flies by.

In this realm where comfort reigns,
A child's giggle escapes the chains,
As teddy bears rally for a fight,
And pillows conspire to mock the night.

Once upon a time, just like that,
The settee wore a mischievous hat,
Inviting all for a merry spree,
Where laughter bloomed, wild and free.

Unspoken Comforts in Faded Upholstery

Amid faded chairs with stories untold,
Every wrinkle a treasure, a memory bold,
A television that crackles with life,
Brings family together amidst all the strife.

Grandma's blanket, a patchwork affair,
Cushions rest where socks lay bare,
Cozy corners where secrets abound,
Whispers echo, they know no sound.

On the mantel, dust gathers like time,
Silent witnesses to laughter and rhyme,
A picture frame smiles with a secret gaze,
How it frames the chaos of lazy days.

In this sanctuary of comfy defeat,
Unexpected joy tastes oh-so sweet,
With snacks and naps in every nook,
This life's a page from a oh-so-funny book.

The Sanctuary of Stillness

In a chair, my throne I claim,
With snacks and shows, I'll stake my fame.
Remote in hand, I rule the hour,
In my realm, I'm feeling power.

Dust bunnies dance, oh what a sight,
Gathering fluff, they put up a fight.
Each corner hides a curious find,
Lost socks and crumbs, forever entwined.

Pillows stacked, a fortress tall,
Cozy vibes, I'll never fall.
Jokes and laughter, filling the air,
This kingdom, a joy beyond compare.

So come, take a seat, lose your cares,
In this space, no one dares.
To disrupt the peace I've built so grand,
Together we'll laugh, hand in hand.

Enigma of Everyday Life

A couch that swallows all my woes,
Where the popcorn tumbles, and laughter flows.
Mysteries lurk in every seam,
Did I just hear the cat's wild scream?

Coffee cups with tales to tell,
Like ancient relics in a spell.
Find the remote? A quest so bold,
Will it end with treasure or stories told?

Mismatched socks hide under the chair,
Where did they go? I swear it's unfair!
Chasing ducks that quack in my dreams,
The couch giggles, or so it seems.

Every time I sit and sigh,
Real-life problems seem to fly.
In this space quirky and bright,
Behold! The charm of silly delight.

Between the Pages of Magazines

Flipping through dreams, on glossy sheets,
Where cats wear hats and time competes.
Each page a portal, every line,
Could fashion tips be all that divine?

Hidden snacks lie in the folds,
A treasure trove where laughter molds.
DIY crafts that promise fun,
Tomorrow's office? A cake-shaped bun!

Suddenly gadgets, so sleek and bright,
Reminds me to cuddle my pillow tight.
As I ponder if avocado toast,
Is a food or just a ghost?

So gather 'round, come take a look,
At silly recipes and a fashion book.
In this stash of whimsy, we'll uncover
The magic between laughter and cover.

Comfort in Hidden Places

A quilt of chaos, tossed and neat,
Warmth is found beneath my seat.
Lost in cushions, odd keys appear,
In this nook, I'll stay right here.

Beneath the table, I spy a snack,
In corners, I find friendships stack.
Smiles abound where memories cling,
In stillness, hear the laughter ring.

Hiding from chores, I take a break,
This secret spot? A true keepsake.
Adventures call, but here I stay,
In every giggle, the world can play.

So let us toast with our cups held high,
To messy rooms and spirits nigh.
In this cozy hideaway we find,
A treasure trove of joy, unconfined.

The Untold Stories of Comfort

In the corners, dust bunnies hide,
Whisking tales of a comfy ride.
Socks in the couch, oh what a mess,
Each pair a witness to our clumsiness.

Cushions whisper secrets of spilled tea,
Remote control battles, oh how we decree.
Each laughter echoes, replaying the past,
In this cozy chamber, memories amassed.

Pillows piled high, a fortress so grand,
Strategic plans for a TV binge planned.
"Just one more episode," we all profess,
Lost in the laughter, a cozy excess.

The rug chuckles as we skip about,
That sunny spot where we lounge and pout.
In this refuge where giggles bloom bright,
Comfort's untold stories invite us each night.

Cracks in the Canvas of Routine

Monday mornings, the coffee's a must,
But sleepyheads rise, oh, what a fuss!
The cat walks by with a nonchalant air,
As we trip on slippers, unkempt and bare.

Dust motes dance in the sun's golden light,
Routine takes a twist, oh what a sight!
Laundry on chairs, a fashion show grand,
'Is this a new style?', we act as planned.

Dinner discussions on what's for the day,
Chips in the carpet, another buffet.
We grin as we joke about missing socks,
A mosaic of moments, oh how it rocks!

In this paint-splattered realm of our lives,
Chaos declares that joy often thrives.
With laughter around and smiles as our boon,
We embrace the cracks—and dance to our tune.

Midnight Musings on Worn Fabrics

Under the glow of the fridge's bright beam,
Late-night snacks, an outrageous dream.
Chips and dip, in the middle of night,
While the world outside is calm and polite.

Old blankets rumple, a patchwork affair,
Each thread a story, a hiccup, a flair.
Mismatched pajamas, a sight to behold,
We laugh at the comfort that never grows old.

The clock strikes twelve, and glances we share,
Contemplating life in our worn-out chairs.
Pillow debates on pizza or pie,
With silly confessions, we giggle and sigh.

Midnight musings in this haven of cheer,
Whispers of dreams under stars oh so near.
With each comfy fold, our laughter ignites,
In this fabric of joy, there are no limits in sights.

Ghosts of Laughter in Soft Light

In the flicker of glow from the cozy lamp shade,
Ghosts of our giggles in shadows parade.
Each echo resounds with a comical twist,
In friendly hauntings, we can't help but assist.

Remember the time when we lost the remote?
It floated away like a mischievous boat!
Couch cushions searched high, it under us crept,
When found, we rejoiced, and even more we wept.

Photos in frames hold the laughter we shared,
Each moment captured, how much we cared.
With tales of the past, we toast with delight,
In this spectral laughter, everything feels right.

Soft light embraces the stories we spin,
In this haunted dwelling, joy never grows thin.
Cackles and chuckles from corners that gleam,
In this playful abode, laughter fuels the dream.

Unveiling the Hidden

Cushions plumped with tales untold,
Remote controls wrapped in whispers bold.
Under the coffee table, a world so grand,
Dust bunnies dance to a secret band.

Cats claim thrones, winking with pride,
In a realm where mischief truly resides.
Popcorn kernels from last movie night,
A treasure hunt, a comical sight.

Behind the sofa, a sock's escape,
Conversations echo, no need for tape.
Books with spines cracked, stories unfit,
In this cozy chaos, laughter won't quit.

Tickle trunk of whims and whimsy galore,
Those who seek secrets will find much more.
Each corner holds charms, each shadow a grin,
In this lively lounge, let the fun begin!

Between the Cushion Cracks

Where crumbs and giggles freely mix,
Beneath the cushions, the world plays tricks.
A rogue coin rolls, a nutcrackers clang,
In this cozy dungeon, the laughter sang.

Old reruns chuckle beneath the light,
Remote warfare sparks a pillow fight.
Lost toys seek shelter, forgotten and shy,
In the cushion cracks, they laugh and sigh.

Chasing shadows, the pets take flight,
Eyes wide with wonder, hearts pure delight.
Funky throw pillows, with patterns so loud,
Hide secrets of the living room crowd.

Each twist and turn, a new escapade,
In this sanctuary where friendships are made.
With giggles and warmth, and tales on repeat,
The cushion kingdom is where we compete!

The Mysteries of Everyday Spaces

Within these walls, a riddle unfolds,
With every shadow, a story is sold.
Coffee mugs giggle, their tales quite steep,
In quiet nooks where memories creep.

Books with faces, covers aglow,
Hide in plain sight where the laughter flows.
Dust motes flutter like tiny sprites,
In the light of day, they dance through the nights.

The clock ticks softly, a watchful eye,
Counting the moments as they flutter by.
Throw blankets whisper of comfort and care,
In this puzzling realm, we're never bare.

Cushions whisper secrets, soft and sweet,
As families gather, where hearts truly meet.
With joy and chaos, each moment we embrace,
In the daily wonders of this magical space.

Veils of Domestic Enchantment

A sprinkle of chaos, a dash of cheer,
In our snug corner, joy draws near.
Rainbow of socks, unmatched yet bright,
Speak of adventures that spark delight.

Stretched out on couches, stories entwine,
With laughter like sunshine on days divine.
The coffee's art speaks of early morn,
While cuddles become the heart's soft adorn.

Adventure hides under the side tables,
In this living room, there's magic that fables.
Misfit toys mount their daring quest,
To rule the lounge, oh, how they jest!

So here's to slips, and trips, and falls,
To silly moments that echo through halls.
In this whimsical dome, we find our grace,
Behind every corner, there's laughter to chase!

Conversations with Forgotten Ghosts

In the corner, a phantom grins,
Spilling tales of where it's been.
Couch cushions sigh, like old friends do,
As laughter spills from shadows anew.

Whispers float through the dim-lit air,
A ghost with mischief, a glinting stare.
He swears he can dance, takes a spin,
But trips on the rug, it's where he's been.

The old lamp flickers, the chandelier sways,
In this room, the past always plays.
Each object listens, keeps a score,
Of all the secrets hidden before.

As I chuckle and sip my tea,
The ghostly giggles get louder on me.
In this space where memories mix,
Who knew being haunted could have such tricks?

Unwritten Stories in Soft Light

The bookshelf sighs, a world of dreams,
Where unwritten stories hide in seams.
Candles flicker, casting their glow,
Characters waiting for a voice to show.

A chair squeaks, perhaps a plot twist,
An argument comes, but no one gets missed.
The table's got rumors thick in the air,
Of feasts and flops, of loves unaware.

With each cup of tea, a tale unfolds,
Of mischief, missteps, and daring bold.
They prance through the night in a dance so sly,
As shadows whisper, and dreams soar high.

We chuckle aloud, the stories not penned,
In a cozy embrace, where giggles won't end.
Unwritten, unfettered, the vibe feels right,
In the glow of this room, with memories alight.

Tales of a Tranquil Hideaway

In this nook, the clock doth play,
Hiding moments that drift away.
Pictures grin from frames so bright,
Sipping tea under soft twilight.

The cozy chair hums a sweet tune,
Crafting mischief 'neath the moon.
Pillows stacked, a fortress grand,
With plush companions on hand to stand.

Whispers dance in the evening glow,
As curious cats put on a show.
A game of fetch with stray sunbeams,
The room alive with playful dreams.

We chuckle at shadows that leap and prance,
In this hideaway, we twirl and dance.
With giggles echoing off the walls,
Here in our realm, whimsy enthralls.

The Magic of Familiar Surroundings

This room is a spell, a world so near,
Where walls hold memories, full of cheer.
The rug, a canvas, for playful feet,
In a dance-off with a cat so fleet.

Posters wave like old pals greet,
Telling tales of adventures sweet.
A light switch clicks with a wink,
Illuminating laughter on the brink.

In every corner, a chuckle stirs,
As the silly dust bunnies chase and purr.
The air is thick with giggling delight,
With echoes of joy taking flight.

So let us lounge in this happy space,
Woven together in a warm embrace.
Familiarity wrapped in blissful sound,
In our magic room, joy is found.

Forgotten Whispers in Dusty Spaces

In corners where shadows like to hide,
Old laughter echoes, a joyous tide.
Socks mismatched, a sock puppet grand,
Pillow fights planned, but no one planned.

The cat's in charge, we all know this,
Chasing dust motes, a feline bliss.
Slippers squeak like a secret cheer,
Caught mid-giggle, it's very clear.

A vase of pencils, all in a row,
Waiting for someone to make them glow.
The clock is laughing, ticking too slow,
In this quirky space, we steal the show.

Forgotten treasures, a muffin tin,
Stashing dreams where the chaos begins.
In this little nook, we all belong,
Creating memories, silly and strong.

Behind the Wallpaper of Life

Beneath the layers, tales untold,
Of grand adventures, both brave and bold.
The wallpaper's peeling, revealing a tale,
Of dancing shadows, a whimsical gale.

Sticky notes flutter like butterflies,
Secrets held tight, where laughter never dies.
The cocoa stains tell stories at night,
Of toast and chatter, a pure delight.

Remember the time the lamp fell down?
A juggling act turned into a clown.
Our hearts are stitched with giggles and tears,
Echoing softly through bustling years.

Behind the curtain, a wild parade,
Of mismatched socks, and plans half-made.
A quilt of moments, all sewn with cheer,
We live in the funny, so precious and dear.

Hours Wrapped in Subtlety

Tick-tock goes the clock, a subtle tease,
While we sip lemonade, saying 'more, please!'
A hat on the chair, a ghost of a game,
It giggles at us, inviting the same.

Shadows stretch long, a silly charade,
As forks become swords in this playful raid.
The couch swallows time, we're lost in the fun,
In this strange kingdom, we're all number one.

A cat naps loudly, a ruler of dreams,
Life's greatest joys are often just seams.
With snacks in our laps, a fortress we build,
With laughter and secrets, our hearts are filled.

Unruly and happy, we spin in delight,
Hours wrapped in giggles, oh what a sight!
In this cozy corner, the world fades away,
In our own little realm, where we laugh and play.

Within the Embrace of Familiarity

Here in the heart of a cozy room,
The dust bunnies dance, dispelling the gloom.
Caffeinated chaos in mugs held tight,
Spilling our stories, morning to night.

Books on the shelves, a rainbow of dreams,
Catastrophe brews in the silliest schemes.
With catnip and laughter, the time floats away,
In these cherished moments, we love to stay.

The rugs know our steps as we twirl with glee,
The laughter that bubbles is pure poetry.
A family of friends, oh what a delight,
We treasure the joy, from morning to night.

So let the clock tick and the neighbor's dog bark,
In the embrace of this space, we ignite a spark.
With every heartbeat, we craft our own cheer,
Embraced by familiarity, it's all so dear.

The Quietude of Shared Spaces

In the corner sits a chair,
Its cushion slightly worn,
With crumbs and bits of mystery,
Of parties it has borne.

The coffee table wobbles too,
Beneath a stack of books,
Where laughter hides and echoes play,
Among the curious looks.

Remote controls on a treasure hunt,
They never stay in place,
And every evening's sitcom dance,
Turns into a wild race.

With every snack and stolen sip,
The room conceals its glee,
A stage for all our antics grand,
With secrets we can see.

Secrets Lost in the Sofa

Between the cushions lies a world,
Of lost and lonely socks,
And crumbs from meals long gone to sleep,
In a land of comfy blocks.

A TV remote, a missing shoe,
A fortune in the fluff,
Where toys and memories overlap,
And laughter's always tough.

Each deep dive into the fold,
Reveals a whispered dream,
Of snacks and shows from other days,
Where silence used to scream.

So here we sit, a throne of naps,
In this amusing lair,
With secrets, socks, and giggles bright,
And chaos everywhere.

Enigmatic Presence of the Flame

The candle flickers in delight,
With shadows on the wall,
It dances cheeky, full of jest,
Inviting all to sprawl.

A witty glow, a playful spark,
That teases us to laugh,
As if it knew our silliness,
In this evening's draft.

Its wax drips down like tales unwound,
Of moments caught in time,
Where every chuckle, every grin,
Creates a silly rhyme.

So gather 'round this funny light,
Let joy become our aim,
For in its warmth, we find our truth,
In each ridiculous flame.

Whispers in the Air

The walls have ears, or so they say,
With giggles caught in beams,
As secrets float on dusty shelves,
In synapse of our dreams.

A sigh escapes from chair to chair,
As pets plot mischief sly,
While thoughts drift through the open space,
With every rising sigh.

In every shadow, laughter hides,
In corners filled with cheer,
And whispers tell of funny times,
Where joy is always near.

So let us share this cheeky song,
With echoes of the past,
In this cozy, crowded room,
Where funny memories last.

Abode of Unspoken Bonds

In corners where socks like to hide,
A network of whispers will bide.
The cat knows the tales we won't share,
While dust bunnies dance without a care.

A cushion that's lost its old fluff,
Claims the throne, but we've had enough!
Mismatched mugs, stories untold,
Brew laughter, as the days unfold.

Ticklish thoughts on the mantle piece,
Frolic and play, never cease.
Old puzzles, their pieces all gone,
Still spark merriment from dusk till dawn.

So here we dwell, with giggles in tow,
A sanctuary where oddities grow.
The chairs have their quirks, like us, oh so bold,
In this haven of hilarity, life unfolds.

Chronicles of the Unseen

Hidden beneath the old TV,
Are glimpses of mischief, you'll agree.
Lost remotes plot their sneaky return,
While cobwebs watch and quietly learn.

The fridge hums tunes of yesterday's pie,
A duet with leftovers that never say bye.
The laundry spins tales in its own twist,
Of socks gone rogue, that we can't resist.

A lamp in the corner winks with delight,
While the clock rolls its eyes, tired of the night.
Crumbs underneath the couch conspire,
To ignite old snacks and a gourmet fire.

In this epic, laughter leads the way,
With secrets that turn the mundane to play.
Each creak of the floor holds a jest,
In our chapter of chaos, we're truly blessed.

Soft Revelations in the Everyday

In the morning light, breakfast awaits,
Cereal boxes hold secrets of dates.
The toaster breathes warmth with a grin,
While coffee mugs chuckle at lacking kin.

The rug, a witness to dance parties late,
Wears stains of spaghetti, no need to berate.
Fuzzy slippers, they form quite a team,
As they trudge in and out like a dream.

Curtains sway, giggling with a breeze,
They whisper sweet nothings with such ease.
Pillows conspire, planning their coup,
While old books chuckle, "What will you do?"

In mundane moments, we find surprise,
Life's little quirks, our laughter defies.
With every chuckle and every sigh,
The everyday blooms, watch memories fly.

The Harmony of Domestic Life

A symphony plays when we gather round,
From the clink of a cup to the fabric's sound.
Walls echo laughter, like a long-lost tune,
As chaos and calm marry under the moon.

The couch tells tales of slumbering dreams,
While the TV argues with silent screams.
Dinner plates stack with memories and spills,
Each bite a journey, and laughter fulfills.

The cat perches high, a furry sage,
Expert in comfort, and wise beyond age.
In this domestic sphere, we live to survive,
With banter and chaos, we truly thrive.

So raise a glass to the quirks we adore,
In life's sweet ballet, we're forever encore.
A patchwork of moments, we hold dear,
In the dance of our days, there's nothing to fear.

Layers of Thoughtfulness

In corners hide dust bunnies, fat and round,
With secrets of snacks they once found.
The couch's a ship, sails made from pillows,
Where imaginations sail, spawned by our sillows.

Remote controls, like treasure maps,
Guide us to shows, through laughter and claps.
A blanket fort rises, like castles of dreams,
Where the world seems brighter, bursting at seams.

Grandpa's chair creaks, tells tales of yore,
Of wild adventures just beyond the door.
Each layer of laughter, a quilt so grand,
Stitched together by the happiest hand.

The cat thinks it's king, rules with a paw,
In this living room circus, what a hilarious law.
We dance through the space, in mismatched shoes,
Creating a chaos that we all choose.

Shadows of Reflection

The sun sets low, casting shadows tall,
On the coffee table, where we all sprawl.
Funny reflections in the framed glass frame,
Painting our stories like a Midwestern game.

A laughter erupts from the kitchen's end,
As someone burns toast, and the smoke waves bend.
"Dinner's on fire!" a call lingers loud,
While we chuckle and choke, feeling foolishly proud.

Underneath the lamp, ideas dance bright,
As dad tells a joke that barely feels right.
Echoes of giggles bounce off the walls,
In these playful moments, magic surely calls.

Our living room's heart beats with every quirk,
In shadows of laughter, together we work.
Turning mishaps into tales we keep,
As sunlight fades, our memories seep.

Threads of Togetherness

A carpet threadbare, yet rich with our stains,
Maps of our mischief, joy, and campaigns.
Committed to fun, we tie silly knots,
In laughter's embrace, we forget all our spots.

The cushions conspire, become pirates so bold,
Sailing through snack seas, treasures untold.
With silly hats on, like kings of the couch,
We plot our escape or just simply slouch.

A family so fierce, in rivalry's game,
Who can make the silliest face without shame?
Every glance exchanged, tightens our thread,
In this tapestry woven, together we spread.

When the day's mischief has finally ended,
Amidst all our giggles, our hearts are blended.
These threads of togetherness beam and they glow,
In the living room's warmth, love's sweet overflow.

The Glow of Domestication

In the evening light, as it softly falls,
Messy hair and laughter bounce off the walls.
Frying pans clatter, a culinary blunder,
Yet we laugh it off, adventurers in wonder.

Board games laid out, with pieces askew,
In this cozy arena, who's winning? Who's due?
With playful jabs, we battle for rights,
Yet the prize is just laughter that lights up our nights.

The TV flickers, with scenes of delight,
While snacks scatter like stars in mid-flight.
Pillow fights ignite, like warriors of cheer,
In the glow of domestication, we hold each dear.

Each day in this haven, a new page we make,
With quirks and the quirks we embrace as we wake.
The fun is our compass, in this messy domain,
In the glow of our living room, nothing's mundane.

Whispers in the Corners

Dust bunnies plot their great escape,
While cats keep watch, oh what a shape.
Socks conspire beneath the chairs,
Sharing secrets with the airs.

Teacups giggle, what a ruse,
As they whisper of nightly snooze.
A calendar winks, days on repeat,
While crumbs tell tales of snacks to eat.

Curtains flutter, with a sly dance,
Sunbeams giggle at their chance.
Old books snicker in dusty stacks,
While they secretly share their facts.

In shadows, laughter does ensue,
As the clock stops, just for you.
What happens here when lights go down?
A raucous party in the town!

Hidden Tales Beneath the Couch

Beneath the cushions, chaos brews,
With lost remotes and a few old shoes.
A popcorn kernel tells its lore,
Of movie nights and laughs galore.

Fuzzy critters weave and twine,
As the old cat lounges, oh so fine.
Crumbs like pearls in a sea of fluff,
Each a story, some quite tough.

Out rolled a marble with a tale,
It bounced around, seeking the trail.
"What a ride!" it seemed to say,
While dusty toys began to play.

Underneath, a world alive,
Where lost things find a way to thrive.
Here in shadows, laughter floats,
As secrets rise from soft emotes.

Shadows Play in Stillness

In quiet moments, shadows creep,
whispering jokes, while the world's asleep.
A chair spins tales of raucous feasts,
And echoes softly of rambunctious beasts.

The lamp shakes its shade, a comedy show,
As curtains applaud, with a gentle flow.
Old frames chuckle at faces past,
Reliving moments that were meant to last.

In corners, silence is not so meek,
It sings in rhymes and colors unique.
Upon the rug, a dance unfolds,
With quirks and giggles, the drama holds.

Timid whispers spin a tale,
Of mischief mingling without fail.
When light comes back, they hush to rest,
But secrets linger, oh so blessed.

Echoes of Unseen Conversations

Among the walls, whispers collide,
With echoes bouncing, side to side.
A lamp laments its flickering light,
As night creatures prepare for flight.

Chairs shake hands in soft embrace,
While vases nod in their secret space.
Remembering laughter, joys and cries,
Relationships grow in unseen ties.

Author's quill dances with delight,
As paragraphs gossip, day and night.
A clock chortles, counting the fun,
Minutes race as stories run.

In shadows, conversations bloom,
Filling the air with joyous room.
The unseen realm is never alone,
In every echo, a heart is grown.

Echoes of Laughter and Dreams

In corners where giggles sneak,
And shadows dance with playful peaks,
Old stains tell tales of silly games,
Echoes of laughter, and inside jokes' flames.

The couch is well-worn, a throne of cheer,
Its cushions hold stories we hold dear,
Amongst the cushions, a snack might hide,
A treasure of crumbs from a midnight ride.

Beneath the lamp, mischief brews,
With socks on the floor, and odd-shaped shoes,
A cat performs tricks, a circus of one,
In the warmth of this charm, life's only begun.

The clock ticks softly, a rubber band snap,
As friends reenact the ultimate mishap,
In this cozy space, we let down our guard,
Where trouble is fleeting, and laughter's not hard.

Within These Four Walls

Here secrets hide beneath the chair,
With cookie crumbs and a tuft of hair,
The walls can giggle, they know what's real,
While socks and slippers have their own appeal.

The TV buzzes with laughter and cheer,
As half-finished snacks gather near,
Each show a portal to another time,
In this small world, everything feels sublime.

Sunlight streams in through the dusty panes,
Highlighting our quirky, jovial reigns,
We dance like fools, and the pets join in,
Making the ordinary feel like a win.

Every nook whispers of things gone past,
Of wheezing laughter that's built to last,
In corners, we stash our moments bright,
Within these four walls, the world feels right.

The Insidious Charm of Routine

Every Thursday comes with the same old pizza,
And movies that never seem to tease ya,
Yet somehow this sameness feels just like gold,
With sitcoms that comfort and never get old.

The remote control is a magic wand,
As kids and critters creep, unplanned,
Trading the great outdoors for a couch,
The best kind of life, then, we vow, we'll crouch.

We sip our drinks in the same old spots,
While the cat critiques our bingo thoughts,
With each routine laugh, the world realigns,
An unshakable truth found in the confines.

Yet every now and then, we sneak some flair,
Trying out new snacks, but oh, beware!
For soon enough, we're back on the track,
Entranced by the charm of the habitual snack.

Memories Tucked Away

In boxes piled high, the dust bunnies play,
Old board games rest, craving the fray,
Each piece a reminder of nights spent in glee,
Of laughter that echoes, delightful and free.

Oh, the photographs stuck in the drawer,
With faces laughing, and stories galore,
Who knew the couch could be such a stage,
For moments immortal, life's charming page?

Tucked 'neath the cushions, a scribbled note,
Words written in haste, a heartfelt quote,
Affection spills out with each crumb we find,
Making the mundane feel tender and kind.

So here we revisit, with smile and cheer,
The dusty old memories we hold dear,
In our secret kingdom, wallflowers sway,
With laughter and joy, forever they play.

The Poetry of Life's Edges

In corners where dust bunnies tend to play,
The lost socks gather, plotting their stay.
Behind the couch, a treasure hunt begins,
Collecting crumbs from long-forgotten sins.

A cat with dreams of a royal spree,
Takes over the throne of a soft settee.
Dancing with shadows, she masters the art,
Of napping mid-chase, she's crafty and smart.

The chair hums a tune, it's off-key yet bold,
Giving life to the stories that should be told.
Each squeak is a secret, a laugh or a sigh,
Echoes of joy that never say die.

Life spills from the edges, it bubbles and gleams,
In the living room where absurdity beams.
Grab your popcorn, let the show unfold,
In this wild circus, every heart is sold.

Chronicles of the Heart's Retreat

An armchair whispers, "Come, sit for a while,"
As laughter spills out in a cozy smile.
The remote control, a wand full of dreams,
Turns everyday moments into wild themes.

A framed picture winks with a cheeky grin,
Of relatives posing before they begin.
Every glance tells a tale, a heart held dear,
In this sacred space, we shed every fear.

The footrest reclines, a throne of delight,
As popcorn kernels pop, it's a jolly sight.
With cushions for comrades, we jest and we cheer,
In this heart's retreat, each laugh lifts us near.

Couches unite in a friendly debate,
Who holds the best spot? The winners await.
As cushions conspire, we roll on the floor,
In the chronicles penned, we live to explore.

Conversations with Inanimate Friends

A lamp blinks twice, is it trying to say,
That my plans for the night have gone a bit stray?
The book on the shelf has seen better days,
Planning stories of love in its dusty old ways.

The table nods sagely, it's seen far and wide,
Guests trading tales while the hours slide.
Each mark on its surface, a moment, a feat,
In conversations where laughter and crumbs often meet.

The rug sighs softly, a welcome embrace,
For dancing through memories we long to retrace.
With every soft step, bonds flourish and flex,
In our lively chats, even silence connects.

So here's to the friends who cannot respond,
To the sofa, the chair, and the fridge which is fond.
In my heart they reside, with a chuckle or two,
Co-conspirators in what life puts us through.

Echoing Footsteps on Familiar Floors

Footsteps echo on hardwood, a gentle refrain,
Chasing shadows while avoiding the rain.
The creaky old boards know each child's delight,
In hopscotch and laughter, they shine through the night.

The hallway stretches, a path paved with dreams,
Where giggles and whispers blend into seams.
Each brush against walls, a message clear,
Tales of adventure that linger near.

The clock on the mantle ticks in its zone,
Counting silly moments with a mind of its own.
Every tick-tock, a reminder so sweet,
Of the fun we embrace as we skip on our feet.

Echoes of joy spill where we belong,
In corridors painted with laughter's bright song.
In our playful pursuit on familiar shores,
Every heartbeat resonates, and adventure soars!

Relics of Friendship

In the corner, a sock, mismatched and bright,
Once a pair, now a joke of the night.
A mug that claims it holds great cheer,
But holds only dust—a relic, I fear.

The couch, a throne of secrets to share,
With crumbs of laughter woven in air.
Remote control, the scepter of fate,
Who last sat, and who's really late?

The plants in the window, well, they're quite alive,
Judging our choices, their green thumbs thrive.
They whisper tales of pizza and wine,
'Don't worry,' they say, 'you'll be just fine!'

In this room, both laughter and snoring collide,
With blankets that hide us from pride.
A tapestry woven with memories we find,
Embroidery of fun, forever entwined.

Secrets of Solitary Contemplation

A cushion whispers, 'The best thoughts are mine,'
While dust bunnies dance, a peculiar sign.
In the silence, a cat lies with grace,
Pondering life's great and weird embrace.

Chips crumbs scatter, a path to delight,
Each one a roadmap to late-night insight.
The clock ticks softly, mocking my quest,
For peace in this room is surely a jest.

My thoughts loop like an old, worn-out song,
'Is it too late for me to belong?'
The duvet chuckles, with warmth, it confers,
Embracing the me that just quietly purrs.

Alone but not lonely, I sip from my cup,
Each sip a reminder, I'm brave to look up.
The chair creaks in rhythm, a supportive chat,
In this space, I'm alive—with a wink from the cat.

Tales Interwoven in Living Space

Once I found an old book on a shelf,
With confessions from a past version of myself.
The stories all mixed, a wild plot twist,
Was there ever a chance I'd be missed?

A rug that shakes off old memories' dust,
Holding secrets from moments of trust.
The napkin's a canvas for sketches and dreams,
Of pizza slices and far-fetched schemes.

The lamp flickers with stories untold,
Casting shadows of laughter just bold.
Every corner's a gallery, framed with good cheer,
Where ghosts of my blunders smile ear to ear.

The clock ticks humor over tick-tock rhymes,
Marking silly moments, both fun and prime.
In this woven tapestry, friendships align,
Each tale an adventure—forever divine.

Light that Sings in Stillness

In stillness, a glow from a hidden source,
Struggling to find its somewhat lost course.
Dancing shadows in a playful charade,
With echoes of laughter that never do fade.

The cushions conspire, they have their own plans,
Hiding odd treasures from faraway lands.
A teacup sings softly of adventures once shared,
As memories, like bubbles, are tethered and aired.

Beneath the soft light, bizarre tales arise,
Of socks on the ceiling—impossible lies!
The walls hold the giggles, the sighs, and the screams,
In a room where reality frays at the seams.

In the calm, there's a sparkle, a flash of delight,
An orchestra performs in the heart of the night.
With each laugh that echoes, behold the pure art,
For in these small moments, is where we find heart.

Soft Shadows of Reflection

In corners where dust bunnies play,
Lurking like ninjas, they frolic away.
A ghost in the sofa, a sock on the floor,
Who left the chips? We need to explore!

The coffee table laughs at our scattered snacks,
Spilling secrets of crumbs and the soda's tracks.
The remote lies forgotten, the cushions a mess,
This chaos of comfort, I must confess!

Light dances on walls with a wobbly grace,
As laughter erupts in this cozy space.
With each tug of a blanket, we share a good tease,
Funny how stillness can feel like a breeze.

So let's toast with our sodas, a sitcom reprise,
In shadows where silliness easily lies.
Every creak of the floor is a song to enjoy,
Embracing the chaos, my favorite ploy!

Subtle Intrigues of Routine

The clock ticks loudly, a spy on the wall,
It whispers of snacks, it beckons us all.
The couch pulls its cushions, a cozy disguise,
Where laughter erupts, and hilarity flies.

We gather like pigeons, with chips in our lap,
Plotting new mischief while taking a nap.
The cat winks as if it knows what's at stake,
Whiskers poised high, ready for a break.

Each show we binge-watched becomes our inside joke,
Cackling at chaos like it's some kind of cloak.
With snacks overflowing and drinks in a line,
The routine of laughter is splendidly fine!

So raise your Cheerios in the name of delight,
In the heart of our haven, everything feels right.
Underneath all this silliness lurks a sweet theme,
The joy of connection is more than a dream!

Uncharted Moments in Familiarity

Who knew a blanket fort could be so grand?
A kingdom of cushions, too crazy to stand.
Laughter is currency in this little haven,
Where even our thoughts seem hilariously laden.

In the living room jungle, we frolic and scheme,
Finding old treasures, igniting new dreams.
The fairy lights wink from their lofty retreat,
As we push boundaries with history's beat.

With the couch as our throne, we stage our own play,
Each freckled puppet—what will they say?
Imaginations dance in the shadows so bright,
Turning the mundane into sheer delight.

In the twinkle of echoes, we dare to explore,
The stories unspooling never felt like a chore.
In moments so silly we find we're alive,
These uncharted paths are where laughter thrives!

Intimacies in the Living Space

Socks have their secrets, oh what a noise,
In a whirlwind of laundry, we find our joys.
Our laughter spills forth like marbles in play,
In cozy intimacy, let worries decay.

Trapped in the cushions, we giggle and sigh,
With pillows as shields, we're ready to fly.
Who needs a floor when we float on a cloud?
Gathered together, we laugh extra loud.

The table's a stage, our snacks the ensemble,
As whipped cream and berries create a good ramble.
Every remote click is our chorus of fun,
In this whimsical world, we dance as we run.

So let's raise a toast, to this living room spree,
Finding joy in the simple, adventurous glee.
For in these small moments, our spirits ignite,
In this chamber of laughter, everything feels right!

The Lingering Aroma of Memories

In the corner, a chair so bold,
Worn out stories, still retold.
Cushions stuffed with laughter's sound,
Socks and toys scattered around.

The kettle whistles, time to brew,
Tea leaves swirling, a scent so true.
Ghosts of biscuits dance with glee,
As crumbs sneak off for a jubilee.

Sunlight sneaks in through the shade,
Dust motes swirl in a lovely parade.
Each wrinkle in this old rug sings,
Of games and giggles and little things.

Echoes of a sitcom's plot,
We hold these moments, never forgot.
In this space where we all reside,
Life's absurdities can never hide.

Murmurs of Yesterday in Today's Glow

The clock ticks slower than a snail,
In this room, stories prevail.
A cat sprawled out, in royal style,
Napping through the latest trial.

Mismatched socks, a curious pair,
Lost in the cushions, do they care?
Their odyssey, a grand escape,
From laundry piles, their true shape.

Shadows play on the painted wall,
An impromptu dance as they fall.
The fridge hums a soothing tune,
While leftovers plot their own cartoon.

Pick up the remote, let's rewind,
To laugh at the moments, remind.
In this haven of whimsy and cheer,
Memories whisper, come listen near.

Portraits of Moments in Stillness

In this nook, a quilt so bright,
Holds the warmth of cozy night.
Pillow fights and popcorn wars,
Painted portraits on the doors.

A mismatched lamp that flickers low,
Casting shadows of long ago.
Board games sprawled with rules askew,
Each roll of dice a daring cue.

Books piled high, a leaning tower,
With tales of laughter, love, and power.
Some pages torn from too much fun,
As stories mingle, one by one.

Here in this realm of the absurd,
Life's little quirks are gently stirred.
These snapshots freeze time's endless race,
In this space, we find our grace.

A Dance of Light and Shade

Sunbeams twirl through clinking glass,
Catch the dust motes as they pass.
Chairs lined up for jest and cheer,
The laughter lingers, drawing near.

Underneath the coffee table,
A hide-and-seek game, quite unstable.
A cushion fort, a castle high,
Defenders armed with juice and pie.

The TV flickers; a laugh track rolls,
Cartoons echo in happy shoals.
In this circus of mismatched schemes,
We bounce between our wildest dreams.

As the sun dips low in its chase,
The evening brings a cozy embrace.
So snuggle close, let's create more,
In this light and shade, we explore.

Soft Murmurs of the Mundane

In the couch's cushions deep,
My lost remote starts to creep.
Dust bunnies dance a little jig,
As I ponder life—a lazy gig.

Socks once paired now make a stand,
Waging war at my command.
The potted plant gives me a look,
Like it's hiding dirt, not in a book.

The clock tick-tocks with rhythmic grace,
While I sit here, in my own space.
A snack surprise beneath a seat,
Provides a crunch that can't be beat.

With giggles trapped in every nook,
This living room's an open book.
Humor hides in every crack,
As I settle in for a big snack.

In the Company of Familiar Things

Old magazines line the floor,
Whispering stories of yore.
My cat throws shade, judging me,
While the furniture stares, silently.

Here's a mug with a broken seam,
Sipping tea from my daily dream.
Chairs that squeak with tales to tell,
Echoing mischief they know too well.

A pizza box dons the throne,
While the apples look so alone.
Each corner cradles a hidden laugh,
As my slippers take their local path.

Laughter lives where shadows fall,
Within these walls, it has a ball.
The mundane turns to splendid glee,
In this wacky jubilee.

Secrets Beneath the Coffee Table

Underneath the wooden slab,
Lay treasures most would laugh and grab.
A crumpled paper, an old receipt,
And bits of popcorn, quite the treat!

Forgotten toys, a dog's old bone,
Hidden stories of things once known.
Cozy vibes in this cluttered space,
Where laughter meets a plush embrace.

The mugs are jittery, feel alive,
Every sip, a reason to thrive.
Running jokes tucked in a drawer,
Keep me smiling, begging for more.

Underneath this table wide,
Lies a world where giggles hide.
Each sweep reveals a quirky tale,
As I reminisce on past detail.

The Comforts of Solitude

In this room, I reign supreme,
Snuggled up, wrapped in a dream.
With puzzles scattered everywhere,
Solitude dances in my chair.

The fridge hums a soothing tune,
While I plot my next cartoon.
The world outside can wait awhile,
Here, it's cozy, here, it's my style.

With popcorn bowls in a stack,
I settle in for my comic hack.
The TV flickers, a friendly glow,
As I indulge in the finest show.

Silent giggles, just for me,
Tease apart my reality.
In this haven, where I belong,
Every moment feels like song.

The Ghosts of Everyday Love

In the corner, a sock appears,
Hidden well through the passing years.
It laughs and dances, quite the surprise,
While we ponder the missing fries.

Dust bunnies take to the carpet stage,
Performing antics, quite the rage.
Whispers of laughter, echoes so bright,
In our cozy haven, all feels right.

Reclusive pillows, soft and stout,
Keep their secrets, but we still doubt.
The coffee table winks with glee,
As we trip over the same old tea.

A giggling clock adorns the wall,
Ticking tunes, oh what a call!
In daily life, we'll often find,
Those ghostly loves, both sweet and blind.

Finding Flourishes in Familiarity

Old chairs that creak with every sit,
They joke about who's the biggest hit.
Cushions plump with tales to share,
Chasing dust, filling up the air.

The rug, a patchwork of dreams and spills,
Wonders if it's had its fill of thrills.
Each stain a story, each thread a laugh,
In this warm space, we found our path.

A lamp that flickers, like a song,
Entices shadows to dance along.
With every setting sun's embrace,
It twinkles warmly, a friend's grace.

The fridge hums softly, like a pet,
We take for granted, but never forget.
In the mundane, we share our lives,
Finding quirks where love survives.

Light Between the Curtains

Sunbeams peek through faded drapes,
Creating patterns, like little shapes.
They tickle our noses, prompt laughter bright,
A game of shadows, pure delight.

Curtains whisper secrets of the day,
As we lounge around, lost in play.
They sway and bow, an audience grand,
To our tiny acts in this sheltering land.

In the early morn, they catch our dreams,
We spill our coffee, share our schemes.
Each ray a chuckle, a playful tease,
In our sanctuary, we're born to please.

As dusk approaches, they hold the night,
Casting soft shadows, just right.
In the warmth of home, we laugh and sway,
While the curtain's charm leads the way.

The Echoes of Belonging

A creaky floorboard sings our tune,
Like an old friend, morning to noon.
It guards our giggles, keeps us near,
In the canvas of love, we hold dear.

Walls adorned with tales untold,
Painted memories, brave and bold.
Each knick-knack chuckles at our style,
Binding us closer, mile by mile.

Laughter lingers, a playful ghost,
In every corner, it loves the most.
Books nod wisely from their shelves,
Encouraging moments of silly selves.

In this maze of cherished delight,
We navigate life, day and night.
With every echo, we find our place,
In this beloved, warm embrace.

What Lies Beneath the Surface

A couch potato takes a dive,
To find the crumbs of a pizza alive.
Under the cushions, treasures galore,
Old receipts and a sock, oh what a score!

Pillows chat about the night,
Whispering tales in soft moonlight.
They've seen movies, laughter, and tears,
And maybe a ghost that has hidden fears.

A cat appears with a secret stash,
A ball of yarn met with a crash.
The clinking of toys, the ghost of a mouse,
Watching to see who will enter the house.

Underneath it all, life must churn,
So much happens when we're not to learn.
So let's embrace the chaos, oh what a ride,
And find the absurd in each little hide!

Treasures of the Ordinary

In the drawer where old batteries sleep,
Worn-out pens make a creative heap.
A paperclip army stands so tall,
While the dust bunnies plot their next brawl.

Mismatched socks hold a fashion show,
They shimmy and shake, they twirl and flow.
Under the table, a treasure map waits,
Leading to snacks and old, silly debates.

A coffee mug holds dreams of the brave,
Filled with stories that swirl like a wave.
The remote control has a mind of its own,
Asking, "Who'll be the king on the throne?"

So lift the lid, and have a good look,
You may just find a bestseller book.
In the ordinary, magic's renewed,
As laughter and joy start to elude!

A Symphony of Silence

The tick-tock of clocks plays a waltz,
While dust dances, without any faults.
A soft creak of the floor sings a song,
In the still of the night, the echoes belong.

A sneaky cat does a silent prance,
As the dog snores, lost in a trance.
Old memories hum in the empty air,
While the lost remote dreams of a chair.

Under the table, shadows collide,
In this space where chaos can hide.
A symphony crafted from cluttered mirth,
Where silence is laughter's true rebirth.

An orchestra made from the odd and the end,
Each item, a partner, each placement, a friend.
Let's pause for a moment; let's listen and see,
The harmony found in our absurdity!

The Secrets Stuck in Pile-ups

Clothes piled high, a mountain of fun,
Every fold hides a story, a pun.
Missing socks in a time slip,
Whispering tales of a laundry trip.

Under books, a spaceship does rest,
As toys debate who wears the best vest.
Dishes invite in a phantom so bold,
Who's washing up? That story's retold.

A tangled mess of wires and dreams,
The echo of laughter flows through the seams.
Remotes rally round for a nightly chat,
In their cozy corner, they chit and they chat.

Under all that clutter lies a heart,
A chaotic symphony, a wild work of art.
Embrace the absurd; it all makes sense,
In the pile of secrets lies the recompense!

www.ingramcontent.com/pod-product-compliance
Lightning Source LLC
Chambersburg PA
CBHW060112230426
43661CB00003B/160